Balam & Lluvia's House

This book has been selected to receive financial assistance from English PEN's PEN Translates programme, supported by Arts Council England. English PEN exists to promote literature and our understanding of it, to uphold writers' freedoms around the world, to campaign against the persecution and imprisonment of writers for stating their views, and to promote the friendly co-operation of writers and the free exchange of ideas. www.englishpen.org

THE EMMA PRESS

This edition first published in 2023 by The Emma Press.

Original title: *Balam, Lluvia y la casa*
Copyright © AMANUENSE, srl, 2018.
Text copyright © Julio Serrano Echeverría, 2018.
Illustrations copyright © Yolanda Mosquera, 2018.

English-language edition © The Emma Press Ltd, 2023.
Translation © Lawrence Schimel, 2023.

All rights reserved.

The right of Julio Serrano Echeverría, Yolanda Mosquera and Lawrence Schimel to be identifed as the creators of this work has been asserted in accordance with the Copyright, Designs and Patents Act 1988.

ISBN 978-1-915628-11-4

A CIP catalogue record of this book is available from the British Library.

Printed and bound in the UK by TJ Books Limited, Padstow.
Translation edited by Emma Dai'an Wright.
Typeset by Normunds Ozols.

The Emma Press
theemmapress.com
hello@theemmapress.com
Jewellery Quarter,
Birmingham, UK

Poems by Julio Serrano Echeverría
Illustrated by Yolanda Mosquera
Translated by Lawrence Schimel

Balam & Lluvia's House

Balam*

Balam is my brother,
but he could be a cat.

Balam climbs on everything: on trees, on tables,
on tables on top of trees.

His name is Balam, but he could also be called
Balam, get down from there!

Balam is a cat,
but he could be a boy.
He purrs when he's told stories,
when Mama runs her fingers through his hair.

Mama also calls him Curly,
and Papa calls him Kitty Cat.
But really, everyone in the neighbourhood calls him
Balam, get down from there!

Lluvia**

Lluvia is my sister,
but she could be the dawn.

Her hair is long and black
and she likes to let it dangle from the trees
whose branches she climbs, to eat the clouds
just like they were fruits.

Sometimes she falls asleep up there
and Lluvia, perched up in the tree,
could also be the sunset.

Lluvia always walks barefoot through the house,
through the garden, over the main stairs,
and her small footsteps sound
like someone letting little pebbles drop –
seeds of birds that, when they sprout, take flight.

But when she runs it's quite clearly her:
that smile sounds like Lluvia,
and the house knows it well –
those steps and that laughter
that Lluvia always brings in her wake.

Come here, Lluvia, Abuelo calls out to her.
You remind me of a song that goes, that goes...
of a song that goes... Now I remember how it goes:
Lluvia is a cheerful lass,
but she could also be the twilight.

*Balam is a name and the Mayan word for "jaguar"
**Lluvia is also the Spanish word for "rain"

The Garden Lawn

One day I caught some fireflies in a jar.
I couldn't believe my eyes, watching them walk
along the transparent wall,
climbing with their little acrobat feet
and then falling once more,
creating that soft sound that fireflies make
when they fall to the bottom of a jar.

They lit themselves up,
but each time their light was weaker.
They lit themselves up before my eyes
until they just stopped.
And in a little more than a day
they stopped moving too.

Mama asked me how I felt.
I told her that the little lights
should always be outside
and never in a bottle.

And the stars, Lluvia?
Mama asked me again.

They should be in the great outside,
I told her,
as I let
the bodies of the fireflies
fall onto the grass.

The Patio

Mama walked with me across the patio;
she plucked tiny leaves from the plants,
split them with her fingers
and held them up to my nose.

Like an act of magic,
the wind at once scattered
intense scents and beautiful words:
*Basil, laurel,
rosemary,* Mama said;
and my nostrils opened so wide
I looked like those little monkeys in my
science books.

I closed my eyes.
Then she placed on my lips
the wrinkled leaves,
crushed between her fingers,
and there I discovered
that all those beautiful words
have a taste
that we never forget.

I wish I could tell you
how they taste to me, the words
bicycle, elephant, love.
If I could just tell you
how I taste the word *dream.*

The Peach Tree

Little Lluvia likes to throw herself on the ground
and press her ear against it.

She'll never say so,
but she likes how the earth presses against that cheek.
The feel of the pebbles reminds her of a certain kind of cookie.
Of course, when the earth is wet,
it reminds her of those same cookies dunked in milk.

Little Lluvia likes to lie flat and press her ear to the ground
because she's sure that
something very important is happening
down there,
and no one is paying attention.

The ants
watch her suspiciously
as they walk along the edge of the window.
They know
that she knows their secret,
but they can play the fool.

One of these days, little Lluvia says,
she'll reveal the secret of the dinosaurs.
But first she needs to hear the many other stories
that happen down there –
stories nobody pays attention to
except for her, some peaches that fall from the tree,
and some toys that lie abandoned on the ground.

The Patio Gutter

The rain was so strong
that our laughter could hardly be heard.

Papa stood on top of a chair
on tippy toes,
like a ballerina in the ballet of the storm,
trying to unblock the patio gutter.

All the water fell on him:
from the sky,
from the gutter.
It looked like he was trying to dance his way
up a waterfall,
a wild whirlwind of winter.

Papa was drenched!
He was enraged!
But deep down,
I knew that deep down
he also couldn't stop laughing.

Papa was a lovely ballerina in the rain,
up on a chair,
up on his tippy toes,
trying to unblock the gutter.

Papa managed it at last:
*How did a tennis ball end up
stuck in the gutter?
Nobody here even plays tennis!*
he shouted, now really angry.

*I don't know, Papa!
We don't know, Papa!
It must have been the neighbours, Papa!*

*I hope whoever threw that ball onto the roof
gets their ears clogged up like the gutter!*
he shouted, angrily.

Since then I've loved to dance in the rain.
Though I must confess
that almost immediately after that downpour
I stopped hearing so well in my right ear.
It must be a coincidence, Papa!

The Door to the House

One day Papa closed the door to the house
and went off on a long trip.
Deep in my heart,
I knew that it was an expedition.

Words became
a compass,
a map,
words became *treasure*
and also *the pirate and the ship.*

One day Papa will open the door again,
or maybe I
will open it first.

The Room's Window

Yesterday I got up very quickly from bed
and everything whirled around me,
and I felt very strange,
and I rolled my head in circles,
and I fell backwards onto the bed once more.

They say that dizziness
is something that happens to you when you are on a boat.

So today
I got up very quickly from bed,
and everything whirled around me,
and I felt very strange,
and I rolled my head in circles,
but before falling backwards onto the bed
I went to the window to see if the sea was there.

And there it was.

The Bathroom

Today, when I woke up, I went down to the living room
and there it was, floating belly-up.

I called out its name.
I said *Alberto*,
I said *Tyson*
I said *Luchi*,
I said *Flaco*,
I said *Memo*,
I said *Flory*,
Anselmo, Anastasio, Calixto,
Archimedes, Delmi, Evaristo,
Azucena, Eulalia.

Fish boy, I said.
Fish girl, I said.
But it no longer moved,
just floated belly-up.

We let it go through the toilet.
We said goodbye, we said farewell.

Black Fish,
Tiny Tail,
Star Sailor,
Fin Wings,
Jumper,
Prince,
Ragazzo,
Blondie,
Curly,
Bermuda Boy,
Teresa,
Camila, Tutu,
Tuti, Chibola,
Rhombus.

Goodbye, we told the little fish.
May you find yourself in the sea soon.

The Doorstep

I cycled in circles on my bike
while Lluvia and Mama talked:

Mama, my belly hurts!
But you look happy to me – so what do you feel?
That's it, it's like pain, but I'm happy.
And where does it hurt?
Here, like in the mouth of my stomach.
Hmmm, it might be amoebas.
No, no, I think they're more like butterflies.
Oh, then you're in love.

Lluvia ran outside,
like she was chasing birds.
I think she went to tell them her secrets.

And I was left to wonder.

The Corners of the Table

Lluvia ran outside
chasing after a white rabbit.

And right then,
as could only be expected,
she banged her forehead
on the corner of the table.

Lluvia sat there
rubbing her forehead.
She swore that the next time
she had to chase a rabbit,
a white rabbit,
she would wear a helmet.

A few days ago
someone asked Lluvia
what that scar was from,
on her head.

Nothing,
she said, smiling, caressing the scar with her hand.
It's just where one day a flower will sprout.

Or a rabbit,
I added.

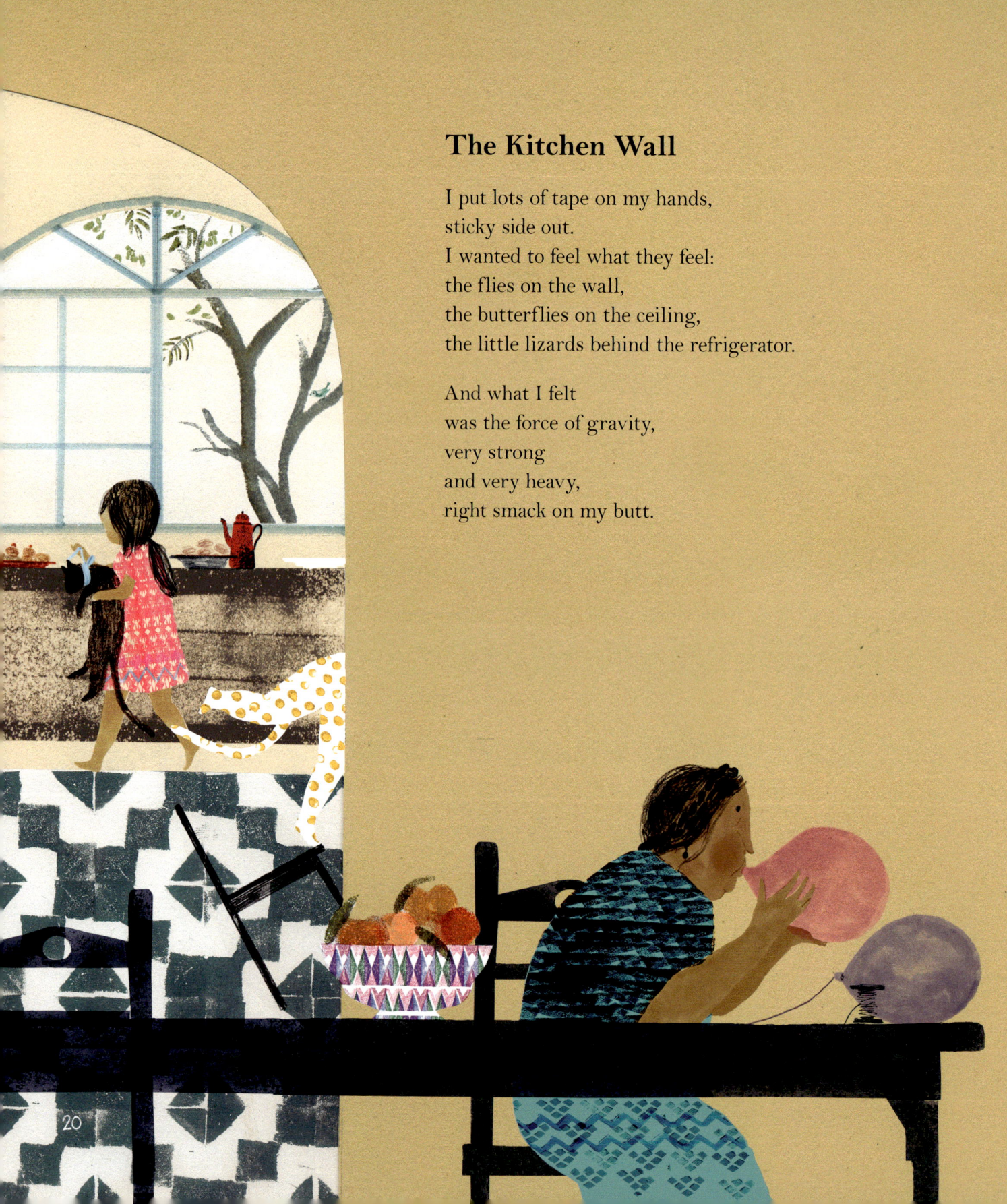

The Kitchen Wall

I put lots of tape on my hands,
sticky side out.
I wanted to feel what they feel:
the flies on the wall,
the butterflies on the ceiling,
the little lizards behind the refrigerator.

And what I felt
was the force of gravity,
very strong
and very heavy,
right smack on my butt.

Under the Pillow

We all know that Ratón Pérez*
is a handsome mouse,
smart and with lots of money.

We all know very well
that this tiny rodent
has an enormous collection of teeth
that he's spent years, many years accumulating
(I think he also has Abuela's teeth from when she was a girl)
as he tries to put together a gigantic smile machine.

Presumably that tooth machine
is what makes us laugh
when we laugh at nothing,
as if something, or someone
(perhaps the machine),
is tickling us and we don't even realise.

They say that this handsome mouse,
smart and with lots of money,
is the best-kept secret
of Mama's little desk drawer.

They say that the mouse winks one eye,
they say that his little feet can be heard
like he's wearing slippers
or running in socks –
that's what they say.

*In Hispanic cultures, instead of the tooth fairy, there is
a mouse named Ratón Pérez.*

The Little House Out Back

Today you're not in your little house in the backyard.
It rained. It rained all afternoon.
Something tells me you won't be there again.

The truth is that Abuela told me
that when a little puppy dies, it goes to Io,
one of Jupiter's moons, a very big moon
for the biggest of all the planets.

Grandma told me that there on Io
dogs and cats share their meals,
and the dogs lick the cats,
giving them strange hairdos.
She says that the cats curl up on the bellies of the dogs
and teach them how to purr.

So I asked Abuela
which of all those stars was Jupiter,
and at nightfall she pointed out to me a lovely star.

When Our Cousins Arrive

Hey! Marco shouted. *What does it sound like when a branch is breaking off a tree?*

It sounds like a glass cracking, Juliana said.

No, it's more like a scoop of ice cream falling out of a cone, Lluvia said.

No! Of course not! The truth is it sounds like the little shriek you make when you sit down on a wet seat, Guayo insisted.

No! It's more like a candy that melts in your pocket, Sofía said.

Like smashing a chair, or pulling the head off a doll, Gabriel clarified.

Or maybe like peeing in bed, or sticking gum in your hair, Lluvia said, giggling.

No! I shouted. *It sounds like when the string of a kite breaks and it disappears into the sky.*

No, because then it would sound just like a balloon slipping out of your hand, Mateo retorted.

Uncle Totó, who was in the yard listening to us, grumbled: *Kids! Those are not sounds.*

To which we replied all together: *Of course they are!*

A Poem We Like

We are like seashells,
that's how we are:
a labyrinth that can fit the ocean
inside.

Tiny,
that's how we are.

Blue, everything is blue but the sand,
everything is blue but the sea foam.
Children who race across the beach,
waves that chase after the children.

Everything is blue, even the children.

And it seems to me
that the world is a seashell.
Who will hold it in their hand,
listening to the sea,
as I listen now?

The Living Room Window

One day, Mama closed a window.
And we learned from the cat
how to get out
without Mama realising.

Contents

Balam 4
Lluvia 5
The Garden Lawn 6
The Patio 7
The Peach Tree 8
The Patio Gutter 10
The Door to the House 12
The Room's Window 15
The Bathroom 16
The Doorstep 18
The Corners of the Table 19
The Kitchen Wall 20
Under the Pillow 21
The Little House Out Back ... 23
When Our Cousins Arrive 24
A Poem We Like 25
The Living Room Window ... 26

JULIO SERRANO ECHEVERRÍA
Author

Julio Serrano Echeverría is a Guatemalan writer, poet, filmmaker and multidisciplinary artist of mixed African and Mayan descent. He has held fellowships from the Fundación Carolina, the Iberoamerican Artists Residence FONCA-AECID and the University of Colorado at Colorado Springs.

His poetry collections include *Antes del mar, Estados de la materia, Central Ámerica, Fractal, Actos de magia* and *Las palabras y los días*, and his children's books include *En botas de astronauta* and *Dos cabezas para meter un gol*.

He was one of the founders of the Quetzaltenango International Poetry Festival. He is cofounder and creative coordinator of Agencia Ocote, an interdisciplinary Guatemalan digital media outlet that views journalism in dialogue with art to grapple with, among other subjects, historic memory, transitional justice and women's rights.

He has participated in many international poetry festivals, and his work is also translated into Italian and Bengali.

YOLANDA MOSQUERA
Illustrator

Yolanda Mosquera lives and works in the north of Spain near the countryside.

She majored in graphic design at the University of the Basque Country and holds a postgraduate degree in children's book illustration from the EINA University School of Design and Art of Barcelona (2008). She has worked as a graphic designer and illustrator, taught art and illustration and hosted creative workshops in Bilbao and Vitoria-Gasteiz.

Since 2011, she has illustrated numerous books from Brazil, Portugal, Uruguay and Italy, including *The Silence of Water* by Nobel prize-winning author José Saramago, translated into English by Margaret Jull Costa (Seven Stories Press, 2023), the Spanish translation of Guy de Maupassant's classic *Little Louise Roque*, and *Llévame* by Mercedes Calvo. Her work has been exhibited in Portugal, Korea, China, Italy, USA, Mexico, and most recently at the Bratislava Biennale of Illustration.

She obtained an honorable mention in the Sharjah Exhibition for Children's Books Illustrations Third Edition (UAE, 2014) and was awarded the Euskadi Prize for Literary Illustration (2018), one of the Basque Country's most prestigious accolades.

LAWRENCE SCHIMEL
TRANSLATOR

Lawrence Schimel (New York City, 1971) is a full-time author, writing in both Spanish and English, who has published over 130 books in a wide range of genres. His picture books have won a Crystal Kite Award from the Society of Children's Book Writers and Illustrators, a White Raven from the International Youth Library in Munich, and have been chosen by IBBY for Outstanding Books for Young People with Disabilities (three times), among other honors. His writings have been translated into over fifty languages, including Icelandic, Maltese, Farsi, Kurdish, Basque, Luxembourgish, Changana, Romansch, and Japanese. In addition to his own writing, he is a prolific literary translator, primarily into English and into Spanish, who has published over 150 books.

His translations into English have won a Batchelder Honor from the American Library Association, a PEN Translates Award from English PEN (three times), a National Endowment for the Arts Translation Fellowship (with Layla Benitez-James), and was Highly Commended in the CLiPPA, among other honors. He started the Spain chapter of the Society of Children's Book Writers and illustrators and served as its Regional Advisor for five years. He also coordinated the International SCBWI Conference in Madrid and the first two SCBWI-Bologna Book Fair conferences. He lives in Madrid, Spain.